Jumpers from the Belfry Tower

by

Ryan Quinn Flanagan

"I will never find the faces for all goodbyes I've made"

- Leonard Cohen

Contents

Confusion is the Only Form of Communication

Sometimes
I like to stand
in the basement
like some hairy mole-thing,
blind in the darkness,
sniffing around
pink-nosed and
whiskered
and sometimes I like
to climb
into boxes
and pretend that I
come with a manual
written in three
languages.

But most the time
I just like to be misunderstood
and misunderstand
in kind.

The same way
you walk barefoot
through a tiny beam of light
and it makes you
think you blinked
when you
didn't.

The Ants Crawl like Egypt,
Out of Desert Sands

Ordering a pizza is safer than jousting on the highwire
but that's neither here, nor there –
what's important to realize is that elephants
(both Indian and African)
are just fat giraffes
short on iron
and that battleships make love
with the sea
and that I would hardly lie
about such things
having sworn an oath
to the ants
that crawl like Egypt,
out of desert
sands.

I Might Need You

It's always the same line
when she's trying to activate
new credit cards.

Somehow,
I am always listed
as the primary card holder
and she as the secondary
card holder
and whenever she needs
to do anything
the voice on the other end
of the phone
always needs to talk
to me
for verification.

And it is always the same:

what's your name?
phone number?
date of birth?
card number?
last four digits for
verification?

Then I am put on hold
while Richard Marx
serenades me
with a song from
my youth.

When the voice returns,
it is not enough
that I am
who I say I am
and give my permission
for this or that
to happen.

I must then sit and listen
to the same up-sell
they've been pushing
for the last ten
years:

can I interest you in our valued points protection plan?
for only an additional 60 cents
on every hundred dollars
you and your spouse can be covered up to yada yada dollars
in case of death, dismemberment, amputation,
loss of job,
can I sign you up
for this limited time service
today?

They always say both dismemberment
and amputation.

They seem rather certain
that I will lose a
limb.

I always answer no
anyways
hand the phone back

to my old lady
and walk back into
the other room

while I still
can.

Flags

Much paucity of Being;
failed transmissions and failed lives.
The rice is burnt to the bottom of Asia,
the gadfly is jealous of the maggot
in summer.
And when you look on high
there is nothing to see
but flags:

flags of death
flags for nations
flags instead of clouds

in the tilted wind
waving.

#3 This Time

He walked into the room
third in line
and faced the mirror
like the voice
said.

It was like god
was telling him
to face forward
turn left
turn right.

Then he was lead
out of room
and back
to his cell.

And instructed
not to turn around
until he heard
the cell door
close.

The Nights Are Long
and the Days Are Forever

Somewhere
there is a party going on,
cheap booze and fine women
or the other way around,
somewhere there are paper plate
Hors d'oeuvres
and a coat room
full of dead animals
and talk of the weather
or the markets
(much banality
so as not to offend)
and there's a host, of course,
you've got to have a host,
a woman slight of build
late thirties
in a blue dress
and heels
making everyone feel comfortable
over finished floors,
eyebrows plunked like apples
from a tree,
everything planned
right down
to the serviettes.

I am not at the party.
I am here, tonight,
with the cosmos
in my skull.

Immersed in my ink stain legions
of ball point
tomfoolery.
Chewing on the bed sheets
of reason.

But somewhere
there are registered voters
feigning much concern.
For you, for me,
for the Shona peoples
of Southern
Africa.

Somewhere
a salamander is brushing
its teeth right now,
with paste and bristles
and hygiene
60 million years
old,
or more.

A Great Couple

I like to give hand jobs,
she smiled
reaching down into my pants.

What a coincidence,
I said,
I like receiving hand
jobs.

Well I guess we make a great
couple then.

I agreed.

Then we made a great couple
all over the
sheets.

Jumpers from the Belfry Tower

Look at the dancing bears
sane as jarred mustard,
see how the cars with vanity plates
weaving from lane to lane
to lane
feel joke store
entitled,
watch the Spanish
(great galleons
of ego)
cross the Atlantic
in search of chocolate
gods,
dip your toes
in the murky shave water
of change-table
benediction.

And the people and the places and the names
and the desires...

There is a boiling
in the cauldron,
a great building
of verve
and energy
and magma
deep down,

deep
deep

down in the mouth
of the earth
where cavities
and tiny mole-
things

reside.

You're a Very Generous Man

I walk into the St Vincent de Paul
along Elizabeth Square
and tell the two old ladies
by the cash
that I have some things to donate
and require some assistance.
A squirrely looking guy
with white garden gloves on
follows me out
to the car.
He is hunched and wiry
and looks like he has a thorax
where his human chest should be.
I let him take the book boxes
because he reminds me
of an uncle
I never liked.
Not that he either looks
or acts
like said uncle
in any way,
he just reminds me
somehow
and that is enough.
I grab two fishing rods
and an old pair of jack boots
I'd purchased from the army surplus
ten years earlier
and head back inside.
As I follow the squirrely looking guy
to the back

I am accosted by both old
ladies.
The first one grabs the fishing rods
from my hand
and admires them:

These 12 footers?
she asks.

Don't know,
I say.

She smiles
tucks them behind the cash
and returns.

The other one
grabs the jack boots
from my other hand
throws them in a bag
and walks them out
to her car.

Spring cleaning or moving?
says the first old woman
pumping me for information.

Moving,
I say.

In town or out?

In town,
I say,

just a few streets
over.

Well, you're a very generous man,
she says.

The second woman is back
from her car
and agrees.

I smile
turn
and walk out
of the store.

Generous,
I think to myself,
I've never heard a woman
call me that
before.

Generous, generous, generous...
it all sounds so very
strange.

Like a sand flea
being told it's good
and brave
and clean

for the first
time.

I drive off.

Pleasantly
confused.

Let's Make it a True Daily Double, Alex

We watch Jeopardy together
over dinner each night.

Her
on her couch.

Me
on mine.

She does much better
than I.

When it comes time
for each contestant
to share a personal anecdote
with Alex
after the first commercial
break,
I hit the mute button.
People bore
and disgust me.
They always have.
I prefer to make up my own narratives
for each of the contestants:

Jude Cremsler
is an attorney at law
from Queens, New York
who once met the Dali Lama
in a Chinese restaurant
in the Bronx

and dared him
to eat a chicken ball
off the floor.

Peter Monaghan
is an unemployed beekeeper
from Atlanta, Georgia
who still lives in his mother's basement
and sniffs her post-coital panties
to internet kiddie
porn.

And our returning champion
Sally Fisher
is an amateur botanist
and proud mother of three
from Scranton, Pennsylvania
who once backpacked through the Alps
carrying a seedless grape
between the cheeks of her
ass.

My old lady usually laughs.

She also snores
in bed
and misplaces my socks,
but it could be
worse.

Did you know that
the female seahorse
lays her eggs in the skin
of the male?

Seems
I got off easy
this time
around.

You too.

Dog Days

Another dog barking,
what's new?
the toilet chain is broken
the fridge is empty
the Padres still suck
all the way back
to San Diego...
a six game home stint
opening against the Royals
on Thursday.
Another dog barking
from the dugout,
ready to kick sand
at the home base umpire,
surrounded by orange
Gatorade tubs
and the indignant waving arms
of 60 000 strong;
indignant because they
make
you pay
for parking
food
drink
admission,
then always get the call
wrong.

The Odds of Nothing
are Nothing

Ever wish
the trapeze artist
would fall?

That the fire eater
would burst
into flames
or the lion tamer
would get
what was coming?

No such luck,
motherfucker.

The game
is fixed,
just as it has
always
been.

Tickling the Sky
with Pointed Thunder

The giant ninja star
tore its way through the rose
garden,
high above prickly rejection
letter stems
of green curse hijinks,
and the glinting sides
of the ninja star
played the xylophone ribs
of the sky   so well
that all the terrified screaming
people
stopped being terrified
for just a
moment

stood up
and applauded

as Antoinette rose heads
tumbled by
like weeds.

Death of the Savage

There are men who live in trees,
wild web-toed bird men
of screaming brown thunder,
men of clubbed women
and twisted loincloth humility
whose mere sight would force the locking up
of a million gated communities,
men of long hair and bad breath
and strange growths,
jobless bearded men named after dusty volcano gods
of wiry string bean animism;
there is that kind of man
and then
there is the other:
not the men who live in trees
but rather
men who once slept in
tree houses
as young boys
during lazy backyard summers,
drinking their mother's lemonade
and jacking off to a stack
of father's dirty
magazines,
the pages stuck together
with dried lemonade
or dried excitement
or both,
men driving late model cars
along freshly paved avenues
to well-paying jobs

and long lunches,
plowing wives who hate them
with the same mechanical deadness
of heavy machinery working over a farmer's field,
wives who stick around for the money
and for the sake of the kids
but really just the
money
while their men
work late
lining up secretaries like bowling pins,
trying to score the 7/10 spilt
with pants around
ankles...

And then
there is the one true savage:
Randy "Macho Man"
Savage.
Died today
in a car crash
at the age
of 58.
I had his wrestling figurine
when I was little
and the rubber arm
snapped off,
but he kept
fighting.

I always
admired him
for that.

Still do.

Raining Men and Women
and Children Every So Often

I have always held
a special place
in my heart for jumpers,
not because I am one of those
blood and gore
internet peep freaks,
but mainly because
I am scared
of heights.

This is not some misplaced
irrational fear,
you see.

When I was eight months old
my parents threw me
down a flight
of stairs
in anger,
trying to kill
me.

But I survived.

And now
you have to listen
to this poem,
shifting uncomfortably
in your seats,
secretly wishing
that
I hadn't.

Are You Kidding Me?

She said
she wrestled in Jell-O
in the evenings
which sounded so much better
than waitress
or secretary.

She said her patented move
was the full nelson
and that
if I gave her any lip
she'd be more than happy
to show
me.

How do you turn away
from a girl like
that?

That's like Christmas
Easter
birthday
and New Year's
all wrapped into
one.

Enough

The air was crisp and sort of clean
and I decided that now
would be a good time.
I dressed and took my shovel
out on the lawn
and started digging.
Not long after I broke soil,
the blinds and curtains
of neighbouring windows
were pulled back
so peering eyes could see.
I kept digging
(trying not to make eye contact),
but I could feel more and more eyes
upon me.
I knew I wouldn't have much time
so I started to dig faster
and faster.
The sweat began to pour off my brow
but there was no time;
no time to wipe it
away.
I kept digging.
With their curiosity peaked,
neighbours starting coming out
of their houses to see what
I was doing.
A few even mustered up the courage
to come over and ask me
what I was doing.
Most the others just milled about

in the street
whispering amongst themselves
as to my possible motivations.

Is he putting in a pool?

Maybe there is a gas leak.

Perhaps he's looking for China
or buried treasure
or burying a beloved pet
that has died.

Does he have a permit?

Some had barking dogs
on leashes
which only made me
dig faster.
I could feel my arms weakening
under the strain,
but kept digging.
Soon I was four and half
feet deep
and had a nice long line
that began to wind
around the yard
like a summer garden hose.
I still did not respond to their questions
or make eye contact
and now they seemed
worried.

What's he doing?

Someone should stop him.

Hey, what are you doing there?

They began to take their kids and dogs
and selves back inside.
Now I knew I was really short
on time.
I knew one or more of them
would call the police
and then
there would be many more questions
to answer.

I threw down my shovel
ran into the house
grabbed my army surplus helmet
put on my fatigues
grabbed my rifle and ammunition
from the hall closet
ran back outside
jumped down into my trench
took aim

and
waited.

The Big Picture is Just Small Pictures
Squished Together

I like to be surprised,
she said,
all women
do.

Well, you must love muggers
lying in wait
in the bushes
then.

That's not what I mean.

We had been up drinking
a few nights
and she seemed
short.

Why do you have to be so crazy
all the time?
she prodded.
You need therapy.

I got up
walked to the bathroom
and threw some water
on my face.

She always failed to see
what was important:

I don't need therapy,
I need garbage bags,
I hollered.
And maybe some
dish soap
if it's on
sale.

There was no answer
and I liked that.
Even my reflection
in the bathroom mirror
was silent.

A Little Golf

Arnold Palmer
before the invitational,
Tiger before the pills,
Jack Nicklaus,
the shark,
birdieing his way
down the back
nine

as Phil Mickelson
tries on green jackets
and John Daly
gets drunk
and throws his 3-wood
into a lake

and Vijay Singh
drives his tee shot
from India
to the Moon

on a very
unforgiving
par three.

Rescue Mission

The door opened
and no one
entered.

I knew it was
one of the long dead
head cases
that had lived here
before.

Then a pen
on the side table
inexplicably fell
to the floor.

I did not
pick it up
and decided
right there
and then
that when I died
I would come back
and rescue mannequins
from department store windows
because no one
should be made to
stand there
in the same place

that
long.

Hold the Cauliflower

Salinger was a recluse,
wasn't he?
I guess that makes it
alright.

Laying here in bed
at half past ten
on a Tuesday morning
stroking my beard
because it is too hot
to stroke the
other.

Laying here hungover
head to pillow
thinking of old white-bearded Salinger
(now decades past his prime)
walking across the sprawling green hills
of his compound
chuckling to himself
because Holden Caulfield
is how he once told some woman
to "hold the cauliflower"
when he was drunk.

I like that story
and smile because I have
just made it
true.

Then I roll over

face the alarm clock
and see the world
is almost eleven.

Close my eyes
return to sleep,
snore
while other men
work jobs
staplers
women.

The Crabs Were Mating with Sandcastles
and the Sea Shells All Had
Postal Codes

...then I found myself among the sand dunes
removing toe jam with a butter knife
and wondering why Pangea
had decided to split
after so many good years
together.

And the gulls would not allow me
a moment's peace
squawking
and nipping
and circling
on high

because something
had died
in the water
and floated to
the surface

while the unfinished Stephen King novel
in my glove compartment
was about to be
run over by a car
just like
the author himself
had once
been.

A Real Education

I remember college.

There was a strip club
across the street
that served
lunch.

And the beer was cheap
and the girls
almost all underage,
doing all sorts of things
on stage
and many more things
off of it.

The place
was getting busted
all the time,
but somehow it
managed to stay
open.

And we were there
front row and center
everyday
for two years
straight.

Eager young minds we were,
we followed the
action.

A real education.

After the two years was up
the college gave me a paper
to put on my
wall.

It sits here
in a silver frame
behind me
now.

Claiming
I am proficient
in things
I know nothing
about.

Exaggeration
is Flattery
on the Loose

Rem Koolhaas
makes New York
sound so much better
than it
is.

The delirious
hubris.

Elephant parks
instead of rain
clouds.

Whirling dervishes
for taxi cabs.

A giant Ferris wheel
for every
rat.

These Are Enlightened Times

...and what would one expect from baby sharks in the tank?
  repetition is expected, and therefore: UNHOLY;
unholy like anal sex is to some and Satan worship is to many,
unholy as Elvis was for a time
before Liverpool stuck its Mersey fingers down its throat
and threw up all over America,
greasy acrid chunks of things: bits of Wales
and Hadrian and some numbered seats from Wembley...
and Mr. Peanut felt ashamed:
ashamed because he was a mister
ashamed because he was a peanut
ashamed because sporting a monocle was
no longer fashionable   (after Ford)
these are enlightened times, you see;
everyone is a humanitarian and no one is human:
kill thy neighbour, kill a million neighbours, wipe out a whole
populace but don't wear fur,
and the phones are so small are portable now
that you can stick them right up your anus
and speak to anyone you want to
with your sphincter;
let's see the Egyptians do that,
market ass phones with call waiting
to assholes waiting on calls
everywhere;
or the Assyrians
or the Romans
or the Sumerians
or any of those dust bunnies
of sour milk-toast empire,
let's see them pull off the ultimate heist:

replacing the human heart with unlimited texting
and convincing everyone you are not a thief;
that takes some doing, let me tell ya,
this is not tiddlywinks for half
pennies:

THIS IS SALTED CRAYFISH FOR SNOWSHOES
THIS IS SCISSORS COPULATING WITH BLUE CONSTRUCTION PAPER
THIS IS NAILING DIARRHEA TO THE WALL
WITH SOME FISHER-PRICE THING ---

and you would question the ingenuity behind the enterprise;
sling mud, cast stones...
SABOTEURS, all of you;
leaky faucets during the dry season,
I can barely stand to look at you right now;
socks for feet, ravenous ice pick fingers,
half-eaten placenta
hanging from your ears
like tinsel,
your miniature anus phones
ringing en masse:

RINGING FOR POTATO CHIP BENEDICTION
FOR BAKED CLAMS
AND SHAKESPEARE

     ringing
  ringing
ringing
deep into the Burr hole of my
understanding,
raising fetishists like pancake batter --
about the sharks;

I took some home in a plastic bag
filled with water,
offering them up to my cat masters
who were extremely pleased
with me.

Bed Angels

The bowman takes aim with poise
and squinted eye
grass shoots tall as clipped buildings
brought to tumble
and it is good to have the afternoon
together,
undisturbed behind closed doors
left slightly ajar –
the breeze the breeze
we must think of
the breeze,
cool and preening and legless as drunken thunder,
culled birdsong in leafy trees
the blue star of the Hopi
cans of soup stacked high like office towers
in particle-board cupboards...

My love my love my love is on her stomach.
Making bed angels in the sweaty creases.

The hollyhocks scream
with purple tongues.

Bare skin
against blanket
is glorious.

Vainglory fans
spreading their wind
across the
summer.

Swamp Gas

He was the second person
within the span of a week
to tell me about
swamp gas:

the damn scientists say it doesn't exist,
but it's a real phenomenon,
he claimed,
saw it
and smelt it
myself

gaseous lights,
bitter orange rind
mixed with rotten
eggs.

Then he got up
and excused himself
to the kitchen.

I could hear much clanking of pots
and chopping

Then there was the sound of sizzling
and much white steam
billowing.

And a very definite smell:
bitter orange rind
mixed with rotten eggs,

yes, it smelled as though
he was making swamp gas
in there.

This will be my life then,
I remember thinking,
going from house to house
hearing about swamp
gas.

I looked at the clock.
It read 11:03 am.

I inhaled
let out a long, slow
breath
then again...

When you are trying to live,
breathing is a good habit
to get into.

Apple

One time
in this small town
I stood under a giant apple
and had my picture
taken.

Then I turned into an apple
for the next forty years;
worms crawling out of my soul
whenever I
rained.

Namazu

Her tits
are hangman
heavy
and I begin to wonder
if all of this
is a
mistake:

the food
and wine
and music,
the anal lube,
just in
case.

And I try to change the subject,
alter fate in the eleventh hour,
I begin to explain
about the Namazu
of Japan;
about the giant catfish
that lives in the earth,
held down by the water god
with a giant
stone.

How big is your dick?,
she asks
polishing off her
drink.

Big enough to be effective,
small enough
to fit in my pants,
I answer hesitantly.

She grins
and moves closer.
Top heavy with those
suffocating mountains
of flesh.

I try to explain how the giant catfish
that lives in the earth
tries to get free
whenever the water god
relaxes,
causing the earth to shake,
and that this is why
Japan has so many
earthquakes.

She lifts her left mammary
to her catfish mouth
and licks the
nipple.

While the pictures
on the wall
around me
fall to the ground
with much breaking
of glass
and the car alarms

in the lot out back
become a choir
of four door
falsetto.

Can Opener Wise

Homicide is too much love
too fast,
can you deny
this?

That earwigs
are just earrings
with legs?

Suicide
is not enough love
when there
should
be.

The wisdom of the can opener
is consummate.

Getting cans of all things
to open up
and share their
boiling
tin man
fidelity.

While the laid sod
takes

and bottlenose dolphins
make poems
out of the
sea.

Another Day, Another Dollar

After we'd clock out
he'd always say the same thing
on the way to our
cars:

another day, another dollar.

Everyone hated him
for that.

They hated him for many reasons,
but most of all
that.

He was not the malicious sort
far as I could tell:
two kids
a wife
up to his ears
in it
like the
rest.

I knew he meant it
as a positive,
thinking it would be better
to make light
with small talk
instead of dragging our lonely corpses
silently from one hell
to another

(and he was probably
right)
but after eight hours
on the line
reason is most often
the first thing
to go.

Balance
ego
and hope
go as well,
but reason always goes
first.

No one wants to be sane
and reasonable
after eight hours
on the line.

Why do you think
there are so many tailgaters
in such a hurry
to get home
to no dinner
screaming kids
a loveless wife
many threatening letters from
creditors?

Underststudy

I come back
from the bathroom.

The cat has hopped up
into my chair
and sits
in front of the
computer screen
with his head turned
sideways,
thinking.

It has been a rather dry night
of poesy
for me,
so I see little harm
in letting him
give it a
try.

I stand by the window
trying not to
stare.

He only stays
a moment,
then dashes off
the chair
and out of
the room.

I know how he feels.

It's a tough racket
with many casualties
and little
reward.

I sit a few moments more
in front of the blank screen
finishing my
wine.

Then I decide
it is best to do
the same as
him

and
follow.

Soon
we will be in bed
together
dreaming of
immortality.

Of mice
that hide
and women
that seek.

There Are –

gingerbread atolls
in the dark crawling sea,
carjackings and bullfrogs
there are cheer squads with chaperone
race cars under a yellow flag
down the backstretch
raving breakneck parasols,
there are *moment of silence* back hoes
ingots surgically removed from their shoes
bird calls, phone calls, no calls...
pine trees manicured
to look like tiny green space rockets
at Cape Canaveral,
there are bed sores, bed bugs, bed pans
(much ado about the bed)
and snoring fairy floss faces
into pillow,
there are Gregorian chants and rivalries and accusations
and counter accusations,
and truck stops with gravy
and mashed potatoes,
there are bullet holes in the flesh
pink clouds like simmering lobster
there are stolen bases, stolen hearts, stolen jewels
and family relations of all sorts:
       fathers, mothers, aunts, uncles, cousins,
        nephews, nieces; parents both grand and great,
there are hole punches and glass jaws
and dog-eared pages of library forgetfulness
and sonatas for piano
and librettos in bathwater

and national anthems
in discounts bins
at the front of the store
beside the revolving display
of $4 sunglasses.

There are mannequins in the window.
There are marching armies into dust.

There is no food
in the fridge.
I should probably do something
about that.

Bag of Walnuts

They were crushing walnuts over the curb,
a bag of crunchy walnut fate foisted together
like dirty bathwater on a Death Valley commune,
cracked shells of shrivelled nonsense
underfoot,
various galling flecks of brown murder
and they, both the them, two young boys of
folded casserole pre-prepubescence
stood over their victims
laughing,
imposing their fatuous will over the moment,
over city-limits and no limits
and masticated tree-grown hearts,
and I felt it in my gut
deep
deep
down
in the
gut
I felt dead carrion
and cold dark feet to midnight bathrooms
full bladders and empty minds
scarab beetle sarcophagi
feeding their way through
the centuries
and the snapped chair legs
of hazy Napalm summers
(don't forget them),
I felt them
most of
all;

doubled over
and clutching at windowless
mercy,
I felt it
down in the gut
where things are most often felt
that you would rather not
feel
but know you must
if they are ever
to count you
among the

once
living.

Xanthin

There are not enough words
that start with
the letter x,
he would complain
when drunk.
There should be more
x words,
don't you think?

Each recrimination
always ended off
in the form of
a question
like I should care
or sympathize
with whatever trip
he was on
at the moment.

We were both 20.

Had both been accused
of many things.

He felt the need to fire back.

I did not.

Cozy is just a nice way
of saying small,
he would pace the room.

Cozy means small,
don't you
think?

I never really answered
either way
and that didn't seem
to matter.

We drank together
like that
for three years
before I moved away
to a different
city.

Got a place
in back the retired
Portuguese fishmonger
and his
wife.

Who stank of Port
and mackerel
and greed
in the

late
afternoon.

Dead Flowers

I remember it like it was yesterday
because it was,
I remember coming back
from the camera shop,
prints in
hand –
strange art photos
of crushed Valium tablets
on black tea saucers
and mouldy shower curtains
dissected in baking soda
egg wash –
and stumbling upon her
crouched
and crying
outside our third floor lift,
begging for attention.
I remember how her knee highs
sat droopy over each ankle
like dead
flowers.

How her mascara face
ran in lines
down to the chin
right around the time
that fine dressed gentleman
with the red sports car
stopped coming
by

as
often.

Flaming Out

Bush pilots
overhead
fighting fires
in my mind.

Diving in low
to trim my eyebrows
with much winged
antics
before I crush
them.

The second wave
is relentless
and I soon
tire.

Laying down
in bed
exhausted
with the covers
half off.

The Greatest Minds of Our Day

She was gaga over Hawking, Hitchens,
and the other one,
I can't recall his name
right now,
but it began with an H too,
so I took to calling them
the 3 H's
each time she began to get all hot
in the frontal
lobe.

Ah, the three H's...ooh give 'em to me...
heart attacks, herpes, and haemorrhoids.

How can you sit there and say that?
she would scream indignantly.
They're the greatest minds
of our day.

Well what does that say about
our day?
I would ask.
Maybe it says we're all just a bunch
of jack offs and bean flickers
and tax returns
with holes in their
socks.

Then she'd really get steamed:
YOU THINK THE WORST OF EVERYBODY.
WHY DO YOU HATE MY MOTHER SO MUCH.

YOU ALWAYS SEE THE NEGATIVE IN EVERYTHING,
EVEN ME.

No reason to take it personal, baby,
you live in a slow age.
Instead of Edison, you get Oprah.
Billy Collins instead of James Joyce.
Martha Stewart for Mickey Mantle;
a trading card nightmare, of course,
but what can you
do?

Almost in tears,
she'd regroup
and fall back on her
staples:

Look at you
you unemployed
needle-dicked
drunk,
all you do is sit around here
all day
guzzling at the bottle
and criticizing everyone else,
what have you ever done
to improve humanity?

One time
after she said that
I flipped back my eyelids
and flared my pig nostrils
(thumb on nose)
until she

left.

Then I tried to remember
who the third H was
for over an hour
and couldn't
for the life
of me.

In the Land of a Thousand Chicken Wings

there are things that
are hard to sell
like yourself
or Deuteronomy
or sour milk;
everyone is so philosophical
these days.
The sports commentator
at the end of the Lakers/Mavericks game
starts talking about parallel
universes.

I turn off the television
walk to the bathroom
get pants around ankle
and let it come...

Sometimes
you have diarrhea.

Sometimes
you get shot in the head.

That's life.

And it will go on
without you.

2 Girls, 1 Boy

I only wanted to have a drink
from their beer
and talk
like they were talking
out on the dock,
I only wanted to be
involved in the general process
of living,
but they seemed afraid
when I approached
and gave me the rest
of their beer
and walked back to land
and things
I could not see.

Then I was alone
just like
I had been before,
with beer
and moon
and stars
and loneliness.

As stolen credit cards
slammed against
the shore
and Eastern Europe
made a killing

and parking enforcement –

less than fifty yards
away –
punished me
for being
there.

Masks

I don't understand it,
it seems only horror movie killers
and Mexican wrestlers
from the 1970s
are allowed to wear
masks.

When I was seventeen
and living
on the street
I used to get stopped
all the time
by the
fuzz:

Why are you wearing a mask?

It's a balaclava.

*Fine. Then why are you wearing
a balaclava?*

*'Cause it's the middle of January
and it's cold.*

After a moments pause
they would get back
in their car
and drive away.

And I promised myself

that I would write a poem about it
someday,
about how everyone
should wear a mask
all the time
so that their smiles
can be frowns
without explanation

if they want
to.

Angry Gus

The old timer in the next apartment over
thinks his dog can read minds.
He pounds on the wall every so often
to tell me to stop thinking bad thoughts
about him
and his pooch.
And his rage often meets
with a certain amount
of accuracy,
which is disturbing.
What's that?
says my new lady friend
on the couch beside me.
Oh, that's just angry Gus,
I say.
He's just warning me
that his cocker spaniel knows
you're on the
rag.

She closes her legs
gets up
says she has
to leave.

I show her to the door,
then turn the volume on the television
up to full.

Then I think of passing cars
on the street

so our furry little friend
will try to get out
and run
in traffic.

This is Why Impotence Happens

The baby
on the change table
is crying.

Who isn't these days?

It seems to be
a very sensitive time.

There is much holding
of hands
and parking meter
reassurance

as Kumbaya
is sung
on street corners
where the bums
used to beg

for
change.

Arctic Mission

The arctic mission
had been a complete
failure.

The dogs were dead.

The sleds were beyond
repair.

All that was left now
was to share a few laughs
by the fire.

And to look around
in quiet desperation
to figure out
who should be
eaten first

in the name

of
survival.

No Bigger Than Jesus

Ink blot handshakes
work from thumb
to pinky,
shoring up cuticles
like silent partners
in offshore
land deals...
and it was not until
you climbed out
of the tub
and began towelling
off
that I noticed it,
a tiny bruise
no bigger than Jesus
on your thigh
above the knee
while I thought of laced curtains
and a woman in Ann Arbor,
of circus clowns
applying paint
to family
albums.

Knee Deep, Shoulder High

There were swimming lessons,
of course,
at the community pool,
but chlorine and orange water wings
cannot prepare you for the deluge:
the torrent   the overflow   the flood

I am drowning in stomach juices.
I am drowning in paperweight expectation.
I am drowning for the punch clocks of Atlantis.

Chin arched
and kicking
with soapbox desperation.

Chasing spring flies
with blue tongued
froggery.

Drowning drowning drown-
ing
vile mystics over nylon tea leaves
children throwing crabapples
bunched tissue in moth eaten pockets
on the floor

      I am drowning in dirty laundry
      I am drowning near riverboat captains
I am drowning because the icecaps
are sailing into oblivion.

Banker's hours
turned to bread.

Wheezing asthmatics
with fool's gold
windpipes.

Drowning drowning drowning
drowning
in alarm clocks and brown water
and yellow snow
and freeway breakdowns,
in leaky faucets
and Farrah Fawcett
and clumping litter box travails,
in skid marks
bad breakups
and Robespierre...

The laughter is extinguished.

The flame no longer
smiles.

I am drowning with cement boot custom
I am drowning for gun shy tubas
I am drowning in pit stain
yellow

because the SUN
has turned to WATER
and the WATER has stayed
the same.

While Geraniums Spit Hellfire and the Knitting Needle Stands In for the Sword

Standing naked
in front of the window –
no crime against that;
my great white belly
slung over the lip
of the sill
like the spout
of a failed watering can
with arms
over its head,
stretching.

As the Shrunken Heads of New Guinea Grow Big as Hot Air Balloons

I walked into the convenience store
and bought a pack
of gum
because that seemed
reasonable.

I really wanted to
give the fire hydrant
an enema
but I bought the pack
of gum instead
so no one
would know.

Then
I went back to my room
sat on the bed
and chewed all the pieces
at once
until my jaw
hurt.

While
the lions
on the nature channel
ripped the shit
out of a straggling
gazelle.

Parakeet

She licks the palm of her hand
                              and a paper tiger
                    walks by,
stalking shoulder blades
                    raised
in the city wind;
          raised high and proud
                              and entitled
like Spanish Armada masts
                    on their way
                    to gold
          and chocolate
          gods.

She keeps a parakeet
                    in her knapsack,
          passes wind in
public...

          Someone behind her
asks for directions
                    and now
          everything
          is
          lost.

Cars in Park
and Lives Much the Same

There was a long line of cars
behind a long line of cars
and no one was going anywhere
so everyone was angry.
Four lanes of exhaust
sitting in park
under an unforgiving
34 degree
sun,
44 with the
humidex,
listening to bad music
over the radio
and many profanities
and jack hammers
wailing
in the far
distance.

Summer construction
is not a crime against humanity
and so it continued.

While late afternoon
turned into evening
turned
into night.

Humanity
forced together

for hours
like a can of sardines,
even the optimism
of glove compartments
faded.

Some converted to Zoroastrianism,
others just got out
and walked
away.

Leaving
their cars in park
and their lives
much the
same.

Stumbling deep
into the desert
where the Navajo worship
the rain god
and the coyote
scavenges for
scraps.

Summer construction
is not a crime against humanity,
but it should
be.

Look
where it has left
so many of
us.

First and Last

Disfigured
by the years
the hours
and the demands,
disenfranchised with love
and work,
disillusioned in a basement
bachelor
in the west end
of the city...

$575/month
+ utilities

while the Komodo dragon
of Indonesia
flicks its tongue
at beasts

and Christ
is re-crucified
at every Thursday night
bible study.

Mad, like the Magazine

The black car
sprayed the white car
with gunfire,
then sped
away.

It was spy vs. spy
in real
time.

There were many witnesses,
but no one
saw
anything.

No arrests
to date.

Enough Already

There is ringworm and cervical cancer
and payphones without the receiver...
and he liked to tell me
about his childhood puppy
whenever he got drunk:
he liked to describe the length
of the lead –
green and
knotted in the middle –
the dense black fur
like the back of a paper-trained
tarantula
the horrible death
he witnessed in tears
as his father chalked it up
to the puppy mill
he'd gotten it
from

before
coming home
with a bowl of goldfish
a week later

that didn't bark
or fetch

or do
anything.

Small Room with a View

They say
a single butterfly
fluttering its wings
can be felt half a world
away.

I think about this
each time the ceiling fan
against my face
is done being a
caterpillar

and wants
to be something
different.

And Her Parents Called
Her Wandy

a mix of Wanda
and Wendy
because they couldn't
decide.

Old hippies
from Topanga Canyon,
they knew Kerouac
from his Big Sur
days
and believed the earth
was flat
because the MAN
did not.

They'd voted McGovern
in '72
and dropped acid with Leary
and drunk fair trade coffee
and ate vegan
ever since.

They read the zodiacs
for guidance
and the obituaries
for the rest.

Published
in a few underground
zines

under numerous
pseudonyms.

Made popcorn
on Fridays
and watched the late night movie
on Citytv.

The kids
negotiating bed time
after each commercial
until it became
too late
to try.

Horn and Gesture

The car door
hangs open
my gag reflex
still works
and I leave some
of myself
in traffic.

There is much horn
and gesture.

The driver is laughing
and passes the bottle back
my way.

I take a long slow swig
thinking of strippers
with nipples
long as fencing
swords.

Saddled with Debt
in the Year of the Horse

Marco Polo
went all the way
to China,
so what?

I walk to the bathroom
sit for a time
often wash
my hands
and return
satisfied.

I don't need the invention
of gunpowder
or the Song Dynasty
to float my
boat.

The port of Shanghai
means nothing
to me.

Vasco da Gama
is an ice cube
in my ice-tray.

Hardened
like opinions
before the
melting.

Clean Laundry
Hung like a Messiah
in the Night

Buddha had shoulders, you know,
burning banyan tree shoulders
that hung like potted plants
in summer
and no one cries for the snake
in the year of the rat,
watching runny-nosed landslides carry our swing sets
and fixed addresses and personalised spice racks
away:
away to China, away to Jakarta
away to tiny sea molluscs
in waiting...
And what say you of modern living?
Of replica food
and no Calvin Coolidge?
Of census takers instead of Gestapo
and political correctness
like a stern ruler over the wrist
of an ever-wilful child?
What say you of sun-dried tomatoes?
Of turnpikes and thoroughfares
and shoddily constructed bridges with names like Coke
or Pepsi?
Skyscrapers are just wheelchair assessable
pyramids
with the mummified ball sacks
removed,
embalmed cats worshipped like
rosary beads in desperate wanton hands,

circus clowns on the high wire
looking to diversify,
moon landings in black and white
so the red fire ant jealousy of Mars
won't hurt our
eyes.

And there is much to love about the world
if you don't look too close,
much to adore and hold
and make soft whispered promises
to:
think of training bras and homemade custard
and cold beer when it could be
warm as piss,
think of long weekends
and short notice
and husks of summer corn peeled away
like the engorged labia of a good woman,
of coloured clothes-pins
and clean laundry
hung like a messiah
in the night,
and the birds and the bees
but forget the flowers;
outstretched crocus arms of yellow
and purple
and wonder...
I'm hardly a flower expert,
but I don't think the begonias
are supposed to be blowing
their flowery noses
like that;

all over soiled shoes
not made
for
walking.

Razor

The razor across my face
is looking for blood.

The razor in my hand
runs against the grain
on purpose.

The razor under tap
makes my sink basin
the surface of
Mars.

I grow light-headed, dizzy,
want to put it down
now,
but the razor in the mirror
will not stop
smiling.

Thinking of Copernicus and Galileo
and Bagged Lunches in Blue Lockers

Took the bus out to the observatory
on weekends,
admission was free on weekends,
walked alone up the many steps
to the top
thinking of Copernicus and Galileo
and bagged lunches in blue lockers
and once inside the building
I took my shoes and socks
off,
made myself at home,
felt the cool janitorial wax
against the bottoms
of my feet,
cool and smooth like popsicle
to lip
and when the guard came
to ask questions,
wanting to know why
I wasn't looking to the stars,
I would slip away
into the main hall
where they showed 3-D movies
about the cosmos,
slouch down in my seat
in the dark
and wait,

waiting until it was safe
to return
to the waxed floors
again.

I Should Have Been in Bed

Ever seen a beetle
get pulled through a sidewalk crack
by hungry ants
in one foul
swoop?

I watched the cunt of my mother
swallow a dildo
the size of the state
of Rhode Island
when I was eleven
years old.

Saying things
on the phone
drunk on gin
when she thought
no one was
looking.

Singular Focus

You write
and the rest of it is
goon shit:
cut the lawn
put the seat down
submit 3-5 poems
in the body
of an email.

Meet the family at Christmas
meet friends for drinks

drive in your lane
vote in the election
apply toilet paper
to ass

as
required.

A Nice Respectable
Human Being

The car beside you
is laced with homicide.

A body
in the trunk
and Motive
behind the wheel.

Revving the engine
at greens
so you know
who is king of
the castle.

You wait
and let it pass
because
you have to work
in the
morning.

You are responsible
with a mortgage
and a wife
and kids,
the interior light
still on.

Cut your lawn
seven times

every
summer.

Vote
in the next election
for the winner
by a more than
a furlong.

Tomato and Herring

Every morning of his adult life
he'd gotten out of bed
showered
had a tomato and herring sandwich
then went to
work.

Twenty-two years
as a foundry worker
alone.

When he finally retired,
he received a small pension
and ate his tomato and herring
full time,
but it was not
enough.

His wife had her gardening.
The kids all had kids
in college.

Bored with retirement,
he got a part-time job
stocking shelves
in a downtown
army surplus,
how sick
is that?

After a lifetime of servitude

and drudgery
this guy wanted more.

He needed it.

Depended on it
like commuters in line
for the streetcar.

He'd been trained
well.

In Argentina They Tango

Trees
with outstretched arms
looking for dance partners
in the sun

while the gaseous rings of Saturn
hint at marriage
and garden slugs
are just snails
without
shells

and the underwear
in my underwear drawer
goes from clean
to dirty

and back
again.

More Equal

They roll out
the flavour of the month
at the latest wine
and cheese.

Safe
excepted words
praised by professors
publishers
and critics
alike.

Commas
where there should
be commas.

A continuation
of the line.

In a downtown penthouse
with stainless steel
appliances
and a toilet that
flushes itself

so those
that matter
never have
to.

Sometimes You Wonder

You ever had Botulism?
he asked.

I shook my head
no.

Salmonella?

Not knowingly.

How about Listeria,
you must have had
Listeria.

I shook my head
in the negative.

I've had all of' 'em,
he bellowed
with puffed out
peacock's chest.
Many times
over.

You must be very proud,
I said.

Then he strutted around
the front porch
like he really
was.

By the Bulk Barn Where the Healthy Girls Steal Grape Nuts

The sidewalk is baking underfoot,
this must be what hell is like
if you don't have a driver's licence.
Nowhere to be
and nothing to do –
a burgeoning layabout's
heaven
like no one this side
of my right cortex
has ever seen,
nor will
ever see
again.

Wrong Side of Thirty

The tailback had many miles
on his tread
but refused to renegotiate
his contract
after a decade of service
to one team.
There had been knee surgeries
and high ankle sprains
and many instances of
turf toe,
but he felt great now,
better than he had in years.
He had a new wife
a new kid
had knocked seven strokes
off his golf game.
He'd had a few 1000-yard seasons
been voted to pro bowls
even played in a Super Bowl.
It was a weak incoming draft class
at the tailback position,
so he decided to test the free agent market
against his agent's advice.
The burst was still there,
it was true,
and the vision of the field,
he was in and out of his cuts
quickly,
but his production
had been slipping
for some
time.

He was still considered
an every down back,
able to take one to the house
now and then –
there were still moments of greatness –
but he was on the wrong side of thirty
in a young man's
game.
That's the last thing
his agent told him
before the tailback fired
his agent.

When he hit the free agent market
there was little
interest.

A few insulting offers
to be a third down
scat back.

He took one of those offers
and plays in the desert
now.

With the scorpions
and cactus
and other things
that no longer
matter.

Fame

You don't want it
to early.

If it comes at all,
let it come
late.

Over an early bird dinner
in South Beach.

Or at the funeral
of a friend
you never really liked
anyways.

It's Raining Pink Slips

I don't watch Jodie Foster movies
because she hates men,
said the queer
on the barstool beside
me.
I love men,
and why
not?

I hate both men
and women
equally,
I said.

Well, with an attitude like that
you're just not going
to make it
in this world,
said my limp wristed
cosmopolitan-drinking
friend.

And boy
was that fruitcake
right.

Big Top

The elephant trainer
grabbed his stick
off its mount
on the wall
and whacked the first
one in the
leg.

The second elephant
would not balance
a ball
on command
so he struck it
in the
head.

Deprived of food
and water,
the elephants
fell into
line.

By opening night
the elephants had
all been broken
and everything went off
without a hitch.

Life
under the big top
was good

and the crowd
went home
happy.

Survival of the Fittest

The bikers
on the corner
sell dime bags
in dirty leathers.

Top rockers
and bottom rockers
and full patch members
until the demand
dries up.

While the mayor of the city
works for votes
and the new chief of police
gets tough on crime
somewhere else

and low level dealers
(pimply faced
and short on
muscle)
know enough
to stand on different
corners
far away

from the real
action.

Courage is so Much Easier
when the Suitcase
Closes

The face of the building
fell off
into the street
and there was much screaming
and wailing of sirens
and the sudden taking of cover
like life mattered.
Yesterday's atheists
were today's believers,
knee bent
munching on the wafer
like never
before,
praying to every god
in the yellow pages
that they could go on
while others
perished.

It was a minor breakdown
of the facade,
turn of the century buildings
slowly eroding
into dust.

A gravitational reminder,
nothing more.

And the believers –

newly confident in their hubris
and now composed –
became non-believers.

Standing tall
as peacocks in the wind.
Strutting down the avenues
in designer jeans
and shoes
as valuable
as the entire continent
of Africa.

Late for English

GET OUT OF THE CAR
WITH YOUR HANDS OVER YOUR HEAD
AND LAY FACE DOWN ON THE PAVEMENT,
said the megaphone
at gunpoint.

We got out of the car
with our hands over our head
out front the Wendy's
near the highway
and laid face down
on the pavement
in afternoon
traffic.

I was already late
for English class
at the high school,
but no longer too worried
about that.

One cop flipped the trunk
while the other
levelled his
gun.

After some time
tasting pavement
the megaphone instructed us
to stand back up
get back in the car

and drive
safely.

King Lear
was never the same
after that.

Hope is 5'10, Medium build, Caucasian

The cat
with no tail
sat in my window
meowing.

I woke up
and had no idea
how long it had
been there.

I watched it meow
silhouetted in the moonlight
for twenty minutes or more
before I got
up.

A very sad
and desperate
meow.

Then it jumped away
and ran off
into the night.

For the next few nights
I waited
by the window,
but it never came
back.

I even went out

and bought it
some food
and litter

so it wouldn't die
the death
it likely has

without ever
knowing.

The Truth is What You Make It

The bridge of her nose
looked like the Golden Gate bridge
after it had caved in on itself
after the quake
and friends
and co-workers
alike
assumed her
and her old man
had gotten into it
again.

I fell down some stairs,
she confided blushingly.

There was no reply.

I fell down some stairs
I fell down some stairs
I fell down some stairs,

why will no one
believe me?

As Gravity
Makes Flooring
Marketable

I am used to being drunk,
but there are those mornings
where you haven't really stopped
for a few days.

Those moments
when you can't be sure
when the tunnel vision
first set
in

knowing
you should probably eat
something
or sleep a little,
but won't

because
there is starving
in Africa

and planets
in space

and much more
drinking to be
done.

Number Two in Damascus

The university professor
ran her seminars
in the evening.

Let her little white dog
roam free
through the halls
of one of the top universities
in the country
as she lead the discussion
on Arab sanitation
through the sixteenth
century.

Her students
all hated her
and her dog,
but pretended
for the
grade.

Whenever
you're made
to discuss Arab sanitation
at 10 o' clock
in the evening,
you could be spending
your time
more wisely.

Most everyone

seemed to come
to that conclusion
before too
long.

But they smiled
and pretended to care
like everyone else does
every day of their
life:
waitresses
line cooks
cashiers
garbagemen
prime ministers
presidents

life on other
planets.

Pray to

sun gods
and moon gods
and fertility gods
and no gods

and sock drawer gods
and Japanese monster movie
gods

and
sky scraper gods
so tall in the
armpit
that it takes 56
window washers
working 6 months
in shifts
just to reach
the elbow

or any other minor
hiccup
of starting block
absolution.

Collateral Damage

The bugs
are different
here.

At the last place
they were long
thin
and raven
black.

These new ones
are thicker
through the body
have more eyes
and arms
are crunchier
to kill.

The last place
was littered with
black death smears
all over the
walls.

These new ones
hardly leave
a mess.

Like it's somehow easier
and less personal.

It's like they're
tiny soldiers
that never mattered
in a war
that matters

even
less.

The Foley Artist

went to work
each morning
at the McKelvin
building.

Running his feet
through rocks
and punching bags
of corn flour
on cue.

When he was done,
he walked over
to the bar
across the street
to have some drinks
with all the other
foley artists

who never made sounds
whenever the hot waitress
walked by.

First Contact

I am not a therapist,
this is true,
but I have to imagine
that anyone
who checks their mailbox
every hour
on the hour
seven days a week
is likely
a lonely individual.

I am thinking
about writing a letter
to the old woman
next door.

Signed anonymous,
no return to
sender.

And watching her excitement
when something arrives
in the mail
that is not
heat
or hydro
or 30 cents off
blood
oranges.

Just Something I Noticed

The farmer's field
was full
of soggy hay bales
left to the
frost.

And some cows
and a pig
and a barn
falling down.

There were also
some rocks.

Grey
and steep
and slanting
to the left
like 13th century
occultism

in western
Europe.

Breaststroke,
Maybe Butterfly

He stumbled down
to the docks
on a head full
of nitrous oxide.

Sat down
in the sand
and drooled
on his leg.

Then
he lurched out
onto the breaker wall
and made the most
of Lake Michigan
under cover of
darkness.

The helicopter
overhead
found him
floating toward
the Canadian border

three days
later.

Another 2:48 am Poem

The wind
blows through my window
with the faint smell
of barbecue.

Goose flesh
on the legs
and arms.

I guess I could be
breaking the sound barrier
or practising my space walk
on carpeted floors
at 2:48 am
or familiarizing myself
with the theories
of Newtonian
physics,
but instead
I am drunk
listening to the Smiths
hoping I have not
skid marked
my undershorts
again.

There are great men
and then
there are the rest
of us.

Recycling when we can.

Pretending
to go to church
on Sundays.

Trying to remember
to put down the toilet seat
so others may think better
of us.

Duck Duck Goose Variations

        going

going

        going

going

        going

going

        going

  gone.

Pasta with Sauce

The gigolo
lay on the bed
handcuffed to the headboard
in edible white chaps
as directed,
waiting like a seasoned matador
for whatever may come out
of the bathroom.

Any woman
who has to pay for it
must be a real train wreck,
thought the
gigolo.

He reached down his pants
with his one free hand
and worked it a little
trying to keep it
hard.

Because no one
likes limp
pasta.

And customer satisfaction
was guaranteed.

So What?

The sewers fill
with piss.

Stabbings outnumber handshakes.

Junkies
inject between the toes
for the first time
because all the prime
real estate
is taken.

The city
is in decline
according to the
experts.

Just as it
has always
been.

A Sound Piece of Advice

She was full of
little kernels.

Like Buddha
with a 27 inch
waist.

Pocketbook profundities
all the
time:

skinheads
in winter
are idiots

clip your fingernails
over the sink
or bust

beginnings
are just endings
before the
fact.

The best kernel
she ever offered
happened late one night
after much
drinking:

lay on your side

so you don't John
Bonham,
she said.

I laid on my side
and nothing
happened.

Made in India

To have a carpet
soft underfoot.

Warm and melodic
like a Mozart
symphony.

As you stand
by the window
and look out
back.

Upon the chipmunks
gathering nuts
and the family dog
under rock

while the factory horns wail
in the near distance
and summer turns
to fall

before
you know
it.

The Million Dollar Question

Barnacle-bottomed boats
in the harbour,
it seems ships have their
problems too,
and the woman sobbing
in the window
four storeys up
is not sobbing for me...
a lost love perhaps
or maybe no love
at all
as the vultures circle high
and ominous
in the dried snot morning
because death is always close
like a shoe horn
or a landlord
and there are long lines
of the disembowelled.

The unemployed are unemployable.
The drunks are hungover.
And the whores are all tucked away
like shining little keepsakes
after a hard night's work.

Scar tissue hangs from the apple tree.
It is overcast and raining.

I step over a skinny albino working a Ouija board.

Asking the dead ghost of Elvis
why?

A Long Long Way from Home

I don't really remember much
of what Northrop Frye
said,
but it is hard to forget
that slight build,
those blond locks,
those thick coke-bottle
eyes.

Wandering the University
of Toronto
campus

in search of answers
where there was
only concrete
and prison
ivy.

Rats of New York

The rats
of New York
keep getting bigger
and bigger.

They seem
well fed.

Attacking children
and Broadway
and women
without chaperone.

I don't know
why anyone would
ever start a
mob

in the five
boroughs.

Ikea

She goes for candles
and nick-nacks
with her long blue bag
with yellow lettering
over shoulder
after finding me a place
near the window
among the throngs
of Swedish
meatballs.

A few hours later
she returns
and I am out of
beer.

Then we make our way
to the cash
where everything smells
of wood.

WOW!

Imagine my surprise
to awake to paperclips
for eyebrows.

To stand
like witches' peg
in farmer's fields,
warding off
evil spirits

just outside city
limits

surrounded
by field mice
barn owls
manure.

Do Not Disturb

It was back in that apartment along the Queensway
where I could never relax.
I lived one floor up
across from a drunken Polack
who always dropped his keys
and fell into the door,
but the doorbell was on the ground floor
street side
and people that passed by
would ring it all hours
of the night.

After a while
I began to hear it in my sleep
and awaken in cold sweats.
Then I would sit awake
watching late night tv
fully expecting that someone
would ring the doorbell
at any moment.

Sometimes
I would climb under
the kitchen counter
and play with the
steel wool
until I bled.

I lived like that for over two years.

Then I moved into a place

where the doorbell
didn't work.

Shangri-La.

Giving Thanks

Tiny tinfoil gods
shining in anger.
Because there are no cigarettes
when there should be
cigarettes
and the corner convenience
is closed for the holiday.
Closed, so smiling ashtray lives
can celebrate friends
and family
and complete domination
over the North American
Indian.

The Sky is Blue
and Lying

The bum
on the street bench
starts vomiting.

Thick brown chunks
of nothing
into the sidewalk.

It has been a rough night
for us all.

The morning feet
that walk wide around
the bum
have their hair done
dress in the finest
silks
talk compassionately,
but I can see murder
in their eyes
(clear as
day),
duck under the
table
and wait.

Majority Rule

It is a lot easier
to conform,
isn't it?

To shave
and shower
and take a job
and a wife.

To have kids
sit in traffic
pay into a pension
lay out the condiments
at family
barbecues.

To follow the script
from beginning
to end

To do everything
right.

Cutting the lawn
flushing the toilet
never once
mattering

in the
least.

Trade Secrets

Remember the audience
but never pander
to it.

Use commas,
but not to excess.

Choose your words carefully
until you are too drunk
to do
so.

Then
you are ready
to begin.

A Place with Much Neon,
but Little Light

She belched
and farted like
a ringer
on the stool beside
me.

When she took her teeth out
and set them down on the bar,
I had no illusions.

Business or pleasure?
she slurred from behind
her beer.

Both,
I smiled
slamming my empty glass down
against the
bar.

The urine pucks
steaming.

The sun
setting
into night.

Street Meat

There are tiny bits
of cartilage
in every bite
to tell you
you are getting
the real McCoy.

Splinters
of bone
and chewy marrow
between each
bun.

Down on Bay Street
they catch the lunch crowd
and provide
a necessary service.

No one
should ever be made
to endure death
without extra
relish.

A Crunching of the Numbers

Churchill
in the Dardanelles
was a failure.

Chocolate
and peanut butter
together
was
not.

Edison invented everything
and the sky
is overcast
and there are more cars
one the road
then Roman-Catholics
in confessional

right
now.

Kickstand

I got a use
for you.

Kickstand
not there for me
as often as you'd
expect.

Kickstand
with that bicycle
for a face.

Heavy features
heavy chain
greasy tin man
spokes...

Handlebars
where the moustache
should be.

A Jury of His Peers
Would Be Mighty Interesting

The ex-dictator
was dragged in front
of the court;
91, in a wheelchair,
shaking on oxygen,
thinking he was fishing
for salmon
off the west coast
thanks to
dementia.

It took the jury
less time
than it would
to buy a pack of smokes
at the local convenience
to put the old man away
for life.

Which was fine with him
since he thought
he was on an all-inclusive
vacation
in Castro's Cuba
in blue Bermuda shorts
snorkelling
and dancing to steel
drums.

High Season

The summer canopy hung
over the street
and ice cream cones
with tourist dollar mouths
walked under
it.

Watching other mouths
on the restaurant patios
ask for the wine list
and a few moments
to choose.

As the ducks
in the harbour
ruffled their feathers
with yellow
beaks

and sailed around
in pairs
like shoelaces
on their way
to fraying.

When the Licence Plate Game Grows Old

There were mountains
along the side
of the road
and he began to think
he was on
horseback.

He imagined himself
in shiny spurs
digging deep into the side
of a long loyal
companion.

He imagined waterskins
and rawhide
and a loaded
Smith
& Wesson.

Then he held up a bank
and all the female tellers
wanted to have his love
child.

Because he was direct,
but polite.

Threatening,
with a baby-faced
charm.

Moonlighting

He picks his daughter up
from school each day,
helps her with her homework
prepares a snack
makes her laugh until
her mother arrives
to take her.

I don't quite know how he does it.

When we drink together sometimes,
it is a trial for him just to get most of it
in his mouth.

This letch
this barbarian
this belching, farting,
fleshy gift card from
hell...

Who would imagine
that he sews his kid's socks
back together
and sits in on local PTA
meetings
in the evenings?

Certainly not me.

One time
we filled a black duffle bag

full of cow manure
drove it to city hall
and set it
alight.

Dennis

His father knew karate
which made him
cool.

My father
could work fractions
which meant I better know
how to fight.

Somehow
we became friends.

And his parents and my parents
became friends.

There were Christmas'
and New Years'
and key parties
before I knew what
they were.

It was all very homogenous.

There were cheese balls
and car pools
and much
wine.

Three decades later,
my friend is no longer my friend
and is addicted to heroin.

His parents are divorced
and mine are too.

We all live in different cities
and try to recycle
when we
can.

Long Distance Call

Report back to the mother ship,
I must remember to do
that,
for other worlds
are just like this
world;
you must answer to your superiors
who must answer to their superiors
or you will be replaced
or terminated
or worse.

No one cares that the pasta water boils over.
Down into the element
rusted brown as summer lawns.
Abbott and Costello reruns
mean nothing.
Paper plates, tarantula death,
church bells from the
belfry...

I must remember to report back
to the mother ship.

Either today or tomorrow.

About Diet Coke
and Desert Storm,
as to the viability
of free range
chickens.

Today

A woman in Quebec
killed her husband
and stored his body
in the freezer.

Another in Dayton, Ohio
microwaved her 28 day old
baby,
over two minutes
on high.

I remember a time
when women were appreciative
if a man ran ahead
to hold the door
for them.

I guess
those days
are over.

E is for Epsilon

Just look
at all these
individualists:

sitting in traffic
going to work
watching the same spoon-fed crap
on television
each night
before
bed.

Sure,
Huxley forgot about
nuclear power,
but he was pretty damn close
on the rest
of it.

So much so
that I don't have to read
the book anymore.

I just look out the window
each morning
and weep.

Yukon Gold (2)

There are peeled potatoes
falling from the ceiling
like starch confetti,
falling like Napalm
into another Sunday
afternoon
and my leg has fallen asleep
(all things do)
and the blowfish is puckered moonlight
(most things are
not),
the dish soap upon the window sill
collects tiny sun
in its liquid green satchel,
prehistoric bird men run low
on toilet paper,
if things do not change
around here
soon

there will be many potato skins
and few
instances of
reason.

Blunt Force Trauma

I don't understand why the Spanish
are complaining about being
out of work.

Everyone here
complains about nothing
but work.

Will we never
be happy?

Must humanity forever
dirty the napkin of its Being
with tiny blunt force trauma
crumbs?

I slam the wall in anger
and something cries
that I cannot
see.

I Remember When Babysitters Got Paid

The landlord comes by
angry and limping
and well within his rights,
but you always talk him
out of
it.

The neighbours
don't seem to want me around
anymore
after that incident with the hornet's nest
and shaving cream,
but you
do.

Drunk
in my underwear
at half past three
in the morning,
falling hedge-wise
into green forests
of mania.

Dropping from the cosmos
and straight into
your lap
so you can usher me
back inside
before the cops
arrive
and certain things

become a lot harder
to explain
away.

Sounds of the Woods

outside my window
tonight,
rustling noises
buzzing winged things
unseen
sticks snapping
the last birds' chirp
of the day.

I get up
walk over to the
window
make out the rock
line
of the forest.

There is nothing else
to see here
there

or
anywhere

really.

A Little Tennis

Federer did alright
and Nadal did some things
and that Jennifer Capriati
and the Williams sisters on grass
and Arthur Ashe with the HIV/Aids
and Navratilova more into women
than tennis really
and Pete Sampras
like a monkey in a blue golf shirt
and Boris Becker with the big serve
and don't forget Connors,
little Jimmy Connors
arguing every call,
indignant as a fire ant,
throwing his racket finally
at a delicate frightened ball boy,
and McEnroe resurrecting the act,
rushing the net red in the face
offering to buy a new pair of glasses
for the inept umpire of the moment,
and Agassi on meth
and Kournikova under strange men
with minty breath mint eyes
in nightclub bathrooms
and Steffi Graf with that nose
and Billie Jean King with
that volley

but the best time of all
was when Monica Seles
got stabbed in the back

by that deranged fan.

The only interesting thing
to ever happen
in the game
of tennis.

Open Season

The boat launch
was filled with green canoes
and many fishing
poles.

Screaming children
hand-in-hand
in purple bathing
suits

expecting something,
like a
cult.

Taking Stock

I find it ironic.

Something
on the other side
of the window screen
is always looking
for a way in
while I look for a way
out.

I know
they say the grass
is always greener,
but it's pretty damn green here
this time of year.

The city sends some kids
in orange pinnies by
every few weeks
to reseed it
even though it's doing
just fine.

There is much dog walking
and birdsong
and access to parking.
The world is good and clean
and full of rock gardens
with waterfalls.

I get up

put on my housecoat
make something to eat.

The razorblades in the bathroom
are never too far
away.

Shipping and Receiving

One cat
sits perched on the landing
pawing at his cat toys
just feet away.

The other cat
sits downstairs
in the dark
cleaning his
tail.

I sit here
writing this
to you
now.

Where do you sit,
my friend?

On the receiving end
as they
say.

Blazing Ramshackle Glory

It's a process like anything.

You only come to it
through much trial and error,
error mostly.

Most never come to anything
at all,
most don't care too;
they date
drive
shop
marry
work
procreate
vote
work some more,
then die.

And there deaths mean
as much as their lives:
nothing.

They are the sum of their
toenail clippings
and a garage sale
the first weekend after
their demise.

I want to be more.
I want to live.

The is much blazing ramshackle glory
to be had.

And I will have it.

Nikki

She was unusually short
with big hair,
dated my cousin
for a time
in the
80s.

She worked with my mother
as a secretary
at a life insurance
company
in downtown
Barrie.

Cried
herself to sleep
each night
and smiled
in the mornings.

Only used
yellow paper clips
to hold it all
together.

A real up
and comer
in a world of
never
was.

Allergy Season

The doctors say
it is high season
for misfortune
and you
cough so hard
you rattle your bones
inside,
your chest tingling
as the extremities
grow numb
and the Winnebago
sitting parked across the street
outside
has a broom
for an ass
and you don't

know
why.

The Yuppie Life (2)

They get up
in the morning
together.

Shower
dress
text.

Barely a word between them.

Head to the coffee bar
by the subway
for their morning
Frappuccinos.

He orders extra foam.
She doesn't ask
any questions.

This is how life
is supposed to be.

Freedom
with an extra
straw.

Together
into the city
until she gets off
at Christie.

He stays on
to Yonge Street,
where the pigeons
are a little
fatter.

On Humour

Good humour,
like good
anything,
makes you want
to:

hear
smell
touch
see
taste

it.

Know Your Market

She wrote badly written lesbian vampire novels
set in modern locales.

All best sellers,
of course.

Autographed them
with a long wooden pencil
with the bark still on
that looked like a tree
signing autographs.

Her sister was the publisher,
but no one was supposed
to know that,
so she used a pseudonym
when writing
and her sister used
her maiden name
when publishing.

Everyone got very rich
(or at least as rich as you can get
hawking books
in the digital age.)
I only slept with one of them:
the publisher.

If you have to choose,
always sleep with
the publisher.

Writers will sleep with anyone
they have to.

And maybe a few extras
just because.

I Could Never Understand Hiawatha

The Indian arrow
pierced the closet door
over my shoulder
and I knew
that history was
pissed.

That the years
had not been kind
to the years
that seemed to blame me
for the tyranny
of calendars.

Brother
unto brother
went up
for adoption.

Goldfish
in bright summer bags
fighting for air
or food

or
something.

Far Too Long

There is that rich aunt
from the islands,
married an architect
pushed out two puppies
enrolled them in tennis school
and then there's her younger sister
(another aunt)
lost a husband to brain cancer
many miscarriages
works as a night janitor
at the college
and sitting at your desk
drunk
one night
you wonder which one
you should write.
Both have said
they would love to hear
from you
though they're probably
lying.

They are right, of course,
it has been far too
long.

I am not allowed to write
angry letters
to the government
anymore.

Putting pen
to paper,
I start with
the date.

The Latest Offering

The hole punch
on the floor
says I'm angry,
but I don't feel
like it.

Four hundred
and forty two
pages later

there are many
tiny white pieces
of tree
strewn about.

Flecks of once life
dismembered
and
now
forgotten.

While
I search the fridge
for cold beer
and come up
empty.

Ask Faulkner

The readership
will always try to soften
the blow.

As will women
and children
and life
in general.

They will blunt the sword
of your soul
if you let
them.

They will whittle you down
to nothing
or the next best
thing.

Crap Shoot

Fishing for marriage material:
something tall, dark and handsome
as they say,
adored by the whole family
(dearest mother
most of all),
something well connected
which is a nice way
of saying loaded
and secure,
with no arrest record
and plenty of quilted nosebleed
ambition.

Trawling deep
into the cesspool,
among the starfish
and rotted kelp
and old toilet seats
with American Standard
stamped on the underside
in blazing two-flush
blue,
you stumble upon a door
and imagine the fortunes
that lay in wake:

a golden fleece
a silver jubilee
something from the
shiny embroidered

persuasion...

But be careful my little sunfish,
my tiny melting Icarus wax
of summer,
things are seldom
that easy.

Even you
of private school ease
and free horseback lessons
can be taken.

Duped
had
fooled
tricked
deceived...

Daddy war bucks
can limit chance
to a mere tadpole's misfortune,
shelter little princess
like a well-endowed umbrella
from the rain,
but this is still a loss
in the winner's
circle.

A stain
that may never
come out.

Think of the family.

Think of the yacht club.
Of clean linens
in a dirty world...

Be careful
when you knock
my little darling,
fall leaves
into winter.

You don't know what is on
the other side
of that paint chipped
wailing door:

swooning symphonies
twisted crackerjack,
maybe me.

If it's a question of weight

I'll lose
some.

Of course,
I'll have to start
with you,
trim the fat
lose the excess,
you know?

Soon
I'll be living lean
and mean
and unmistakably
single

again.

Two Heads

on
one shelf:

Buddha
at one end,
chocolate brown
and serene.

An off-white bust
of Stalin
at the other.

Telling me
that his father
was a cobbler
and that it is important
to own a good pair
of boots.

That Buddha
never went to Georgia
where you need to kick
skulls in
to get anything
done

and require
a good pair of boots
to do
that.

Finger Puppets with a Foot Fetish Because They Can

To say things
in an original voice
in an original
way...

I can't remember
the last time
I finger fucked
a cheery-red
peacock

at
half past
New
Years.

Can
you?

A Disgusting Individual

My mother
walks in on me
doing my thing
and calls me a disgusting
individual.

It's funny
how I had to listen to her
be slammed into a headboard
for over a decade
growing up
and walked in on her
shoving a glass dildo
up her ass
one time
when I was
eleven
and I'm still supposed
to think of her
as a mother.

I've met prostitutes
that do less
than my mother.

They seem put off
when I tell them
as much.

Life on Other Planets
Can't be Much Worse
Than This

They spilt oil again
but no one cried
because they confused it
with spilt milk
and belt buckles
tend to learn their
lessons well
and when jobs were lost
they summed it up
to the economy
and when the scallops
washed ashore
polluted,
they ordered
steak.

Never wanting
to think badly
of human progress:

of fire
and the wheel

of Edison
Einstein
and pasta provolone
in under three
minutes.

Even as the welfare check
at the end of every
month
made them wrap newborns
in ratty old hand towels
still caked dry
with waste.
Championing the virtues
of baked macaroni

for breakfast
lunch

and
dinner.

No Substitute

Never one to discriminate,
I spend a lot of time
with people who rub margarine
all over themselves.

Usually married couples
trying to spice things
up.

One of them
(a bachelor this time)
tells me
he likes to think
of feral cats
ripping at old cardboard
while he does
it.

I don't know what to say
to that
so I drink my beer
in silence.

Thinking,
I should really start drinking
with people
who use real
butter.

Remembered as a Modernist

Dirty cops, dirty tricks, dirty Sanchez...
and you begin to wonder why
they even have a clean cycle
as Duran Duran
never leaves the 80s
and unicycles
go it alone

and Peter the Great
becomes an amateur
dentist

terrorising all
of mother Russia
in a brand new
way.

Jumper Cables

connected in winter
over a bridge
along a country road
where the teenagers
stop to
make out.

Connected
to nipples
that believe
in an afterlife
or they wouldn't
be doing
this.

The Ground Opens Up
and the World
Confesses

Look at those earthquakes
there on the news,
between 6.5 and 8.5
on the Richter
scale,
smiling at me
through twisted city streets
where people used to give change
put on their indicators
wait for buses...

Now they are lost as easily as thumbtacks
and the newswoman
is pretending to be distraught
between many long pauses
and teleprompter clichés
when in reality,
she has a hot date tonight
and is really excited
and can't wait
to get home
change into something more comfortable
put in her diaphragm
and go to dinner

in the
city.

Raised in England,
Lost a Father to Suicide

She taught a creative writing class
at the university.

Was well versed in her
rhyme and meter.

She also taught Modern
Canadian Literature,
which meant she sold
her friends' books
for top dollar
to unsuspecting
freshmen.

Who,
with bright eyes
and open binders,
made her feel
like she wasn't pushing sixty

and a complete
failure.

Look Great. Feel Great.

The shooting victim
lay in the middle of the street
taped off
while investigators
surveyed the
scene.

A lifeless mass
of flesh
in bright red Reeboks
that looked like Mars
had a Siamese
twin

from a
distance.

The Trick is They Toast the Bun

We lie in bed for a week,
but not for peace.

We lie in bed
hungover
thinking of meatball
sandwiches.

When the week is up,
we shower
and dress
and go back
to work.

Doing something useless
for someone worthless
until we can get back
to the bottle
again.

Hard Eight

The gambler knows they are destined to lose,
I believe this,
but it's how you get there
that fans the flames,
not some sweet little clementine hope
of victory,
but rather a hard eight down the avenue,
letting it ride,
pushing rent money across the felt green threshold
into oncoming traffic
like watching your own beheading
over potato chips and chocolate milk apathy.
All for that rush, that instant before the blade drops
and you are separated from your body of work
and left with crusty hand towels
and vomit-swirled pillow
mints

and the long drive
back
thinking up stories to tell
the wife
who will want a description
of the knife-wielding
muggers

that jacked
you.

The Moment You Realize

I did not want to work at the sub place
anymore.
They made you wear a uniform
with a high collar
and walk up two flights of stairs
to punch in.
Someone asked for extra onions
and I have never liked
onions
and soon
I found myself
tossing trays of greens
everywhere
stroking off all the fresh
baked bread
during dinner hour
and overturning any of the tables
that weren't bolted
to the wall.

It felt great.

To finally let it out
after so many
years.

A few blocks on,
I unzipped
and started pissing
on a mailbox
by a bus

stop.

The bus
couldn't come fast enough
for all the rest,
let me tell
you.

Rent be damned,
I had my moment.

Dita Von Teese

There is nothing worse
than false advertising.

That's just a fancy way
of saying:
lying.

And it appears contagious.
Everyone does it.
Men do it.
Women do it.
Even the family dog
plays dead for treats.

And then there's that
Dita Von Teese.
Bent over in leathers
on the cover of Legs
magazine,
putting on airs
playing to the camera
pretending to be what a man
wants or needs
when she is anything
but.

It's all a facade,
the whole damn
enterprise.

And there's Dita Von Tesse

rouged up
with black riding crop
in hand.

Dreaming of three kids
a two car garage
and a blue
minivan.

Lonely Socks
with No Place to Go

You just keep writing,
you don't know
why,
eating French fries
with a tuning fork
under the yellow vomit sun
and the Sasquatch of the Pacific Northwest
is unproven
and the warm body in bed beside you
says she loves you,
as for the rest of it,
your guess
is as good as
mine...

I am not a frequenter of crystal balls.
I am not a wise man of frankincense
and myrrh.
I am not some bearded swami
out of the back streets
of Lahore,
I do not dance with bespeckled cobras
in the cotton armpits
of forever.

I am lost to wonder,
and better for it.
Confused by dry toothpaste
and lonely socks
with no place to go.

REJOICE! REJOICE!
in the wheel well turning,
the mating cycle of the giant sloth...

Booming thunder
that reminds you how small
you are;
makes you jump and start
in bed
even though you know
it's coming.

Thinking of Laika

Methinks
the Spring gutters be filled
with leaves,
that long walks in the countryside
mustn't be trod with tired
Wordsworth feet.

Me also
thinks
I should stop talking
like an asshole
or I might
stay

this
way.

Like the first dog
to chase
its own
tail

in
space.

Erasers in a Pencil Case

The cops
learn to fear
the nice weather.

Everyone
is out on the streets
and the crime rate
shoots up
by as much as
40%.

Rapes
robberies
assault
murder...

Humanity
squished together
like erasers
in a pencil
case.

Poor
armed
and dehydrated.

Trying to pay bills
and save face.

Trying
to erase

one another
off the face of the earth
forever
with guns
knives
tire irons

and
chains.

Rank and File

No shortage of scamps
flim flams
hucksters
cons.

Everyone
is trying to make it
and no one
knows

quite
how.

Post-Colonial

Post-colonial literature
always seemed
a little funny
to me.

Why describe
the slavery of the past
when you can live
the slavery of
today?

And to make it
such a colour
thing:

sure
the blacks
have had it far worse
than most,
but they don't hold
a monopoly
on suffering.

We can all work
long hours
for a pittance
and come home
to nothing,

trust
me.

Memory is a Persistent Old Maid

I remember
standing in the kitchen
of that basement apartment
along Evans Avenue
and being so drunk
that I forgot I was holding
a beer
releasing my grip
and simply dropping it
on the
linoleum.

I remember the shattering of glass
and much pretending
like it had slipped
out of my
hand.

Then I had a new beer
and something happened
to that.

And the one
after that
and the one
after that...

And there was quite
the hangover
in the morning.

I definitely remember
that.

They Really Pile It On, Don't They?

I feel bad enough already,
but then there's the
weather,
rainy and overcast
like they're seeding the clouds
again,
heavy slow oblongs
of water
falling almost as an afterthought
against the window
screen.
Inside, I am blowing mucus
into a tissue
already wet with sickness,
trying to stay warm
with heat pads
under blanket.

As the cat
asks for treats
and the barometer
by the door
plummets
and the voice
from the radio
tells me
I:

never did nothin'
to save my doggone
soul.

What Can You Do?

She had a moustache
which meant
she could never be
Miss America,
and that made her
angry.

She cursed
and threw plates
and experimented with
many creams.

Her mother was disappointed,
but they were Italian
so it was half
expected.

A moustache is a sign of character
in some cultures,
I would say.
It denotes status and virility
and all that...

We weren't together
that long.

I have never been
a sweet talker.

She cried
most the time

we were together,
but I don't think
it was my
fault.

Pork and Beans

No respect
for the streaker
in a men's
shelter.

No one
wants to see
that.

Along Princess
Street
in Kingston,
ten o'clock
curfew.

Louse checks
every Thursday
while the men stand around
bumming smokes
by the picnic table
out back.

Throwing peanuts
to ever brazen squirrels,
both grey

and
black.

One of the Boys

He knew that no one
at the bar
cared a lick about poetry
so he told them
he was a roofer
and calloused his hands
with sandpaper.

He wore steel toed boots
and would roll around
in the dirt
before coming
in.

Watched sports on the television
above the bar
and belched out the alphabet
in cold beer baritone.

And no one knew
he got off
on Wordsworth
instead of girl-on-girl
porn

like the rest
of them.

Briar

She is a biologist
which means she wasn't smart enough
to be a chemist,
but makes more than
a physicist.
Both her parents
were teachers in the Barrie
public school system
and she had a twin sister
who was never quite
as good,
with the boys
or the parents.

I haven't spoken to either
of them
in over twenty
years.

Knowing
blood is thicker
than water
and science is thicker
in the head

than
most.

I Must Confess

You hear so many nowadays
saying themselves
(or others of
their ilk)
write "confessional" poems
or that "confessional" poetry
is where it's
at.

I don't even know
what "confessional" poetry
is
(perhaps this will be considered
a "confessional" poem,
I do not know),
but I must tell you
whenever they speak of poems
being "confessional"
I grow a little squeamish
and uneasy.
A dull pain invades
my gut.
"Confessional,"
it all sounds so whiny
and involved.
Like talking a recent breakup
out of suicide
at four in the morning
or keeping a diary
like a twelve year old girl.
Confessional...confessional...confessional;

I am reminded of catholic mass
and wooden boxes with a priest on the other side
of the screen
while they talk about how they cussed out
their mother
a few weeks back
or stole apples from the local grocers
or had impure thoughts
about the Gila monster
of Sonora...

It just sounds like
a whole lot of whining
and complaining
to me
and something
I'd much rather not
be a part of
in any way, shape
or form

if I can
help
it.

The Balkans

The tinderbox of Europe
they call it,
so what?

We need more fire
everywhere.

There are now officially
eight billion people
on this earth
and I can count
the number of living
on one hand.

More than half of them
are cats.

It does not look
promising.

Goldfish in Lonely Bowls

The airmen retuned
from the latest
raid.

Bragging about
the number of people
they had just
killed.

Men, women and children,
goldfish in lonely
bowls...

All this talk of murder
and massacre
made the working girls
hot.

Hand jobs
and blowjobs
exploding like bombs
dropped
before a price
could even be negotiated.

New puddles
spurted out
on the barroom floor
before the ones before
had time to set.

Then a lone bomber pilot
came in with pictures
from his latest
sortie.

And the bartender
(drunk with
patriotism)
pour one 'round
on the house.

For Two Months

Every day
was exactly
the same.

Drive west
to Markham Road
stop for gas
at the pumps
on the north end
of the street
across from the good
breakfast place
where all the truckers
on their way to Ajax
and Whitby
and Cornwall
went.

Pay with the gas card
then drive west along the 401
to the 400 North
to Barrie.

Unload
drive back
stop at the same station
for petrol
for the drive
back in.

Note the kilometres

and the gas gauge
and any outstanding
safety issues.

Fill out the job order
wait for my father
catch the 501 Shepherd bus
back home

after transferring
at Warden.

The Way of It

The fox cubs
were supposed to stay close
to the den,
but they were
curious.

The hawk circled high
in the sky above.

Field mice
wise to the hustle
but still hungry
ventured
out.

The hawk circled high
in the sky above.

Spawning season
was in full swing
and the shallows swelled
with fish.

The hawk circled high
in the sky above.

The hawk circled high
in the sky above
while man
on the ground below
raised his gun
took aim
and fired.

Jules Verne

wanted to be
Victor Hugo
without the
jacket.

When he couldn't
be Victor Hugo,
he wrote about
the future
to forget about
the past.

Then he was shot
one day
and died
and his writing
really tapered off

after that.

I Remember Now

Those were some high scoring
affairs.

Those Florida/Florida State
games.

Coach Bowden
and coach Spurrier
both trying to run up
the score.

But they weren't
alone.

The SEC games
all had crazy scores
like 66-49.

Every Saturday
they'd light up the
scoreboard.

Made you wonder
why they even put a defense
on the field.

I remember thinking that
when I was fifteen.

I remember thinking
there should be no defenses

and everyone should just play offense
and score at will.

Then I remember
deciding to make everyone
think I was crazy
so I would never have
to say excuse me
or shake anyone's hand
or sit with them
in parks
on benches
watching birds
a little long

in the
wing.

Receiving End

The hotel
by the water
was always in high
demand.

It was right downtown
by all the best restaurants
and shopping
and less than an hour
from the
border.

Every summer
rich fat Americans
would waddle into port
and stay a few
nights.

Leaving
with some clothes
indigestion

and nothing
to declare.

New Carpets

I can't get new carpets.

The cats keep pissing on them.

By the time I notice,
it has dried
and soaked through
permanent.

And no amount of washing
will ever get rid
of it.

Like the
truth.

Canadian Winters

The baseboard heater
is never enough.
My legs grow goose-fleshed
and my arms
the same.
Soon,
I am one big dimple
in a world
of dimples.
Rolling over in bed
from side to
side
under the covers
at 850 + utilities,
playing with the pillows
trying to get
comfortable

so life on this planet
is able to dream
and the day
can end
in
sleep.

Ye of Little Faith

The Catholics are afraid
to drive with the top down,
and is it any wonder?
Repent for this, contrition that
bleeding stigmata holes through the dermis
when all you wanted
was free parking.

I drink in the evenings,
only work
when I have to,
enough to cover the
basic functions.

A religionist I know
says I'm going straight to hell,
but I'm beginning to think
such proclamations
are more for him
than me.

Sometimes
when I'm drunk
I call him up
and tell him
I am dizzy
with the blood
of Christ.

Then
I hang up

and watch late night tv
where everything is
a miracle
for three easy payments
and can be shipped
right to your door
in 6 to 8
weeks.

On Evenings Such as This

I like to stare
at the chopped credit cards
in a sandwich bag
on the opposing wall
and think about
how much closer
I am
to finally being able
to say
that I don't
owe anyone
anything

at interest

and can
finally

start
living.

June Bugs

They were everywhere
for a short time.

Usually
between late May
and early
July.

Against the window screen
in your shoes
stuck to heaven
in your
hair.

For a few months of the year
they were more prevalent
than zits.

I remember being fourteen years old
and having to run from
the house
to the car
as a family
and having to ring out
your hair and clothing
before you got in
so your father wouldn't have to kill
something
on the way to
dinner.

Chinese
was up the street,
but we often went
for burgers
across town.

My father would order
as my mother
stood over his shoulder
waiting to correct him
with purse in hand
while my brother
and I
played a video game
in the middle of the room
that only took
quarters
and the bugs
invading Essa Road
like a biblical
plague
made a window
full of wings
that wanted mustard
relish
ketchup
everything

on their
burger.

Hap Hap Happy!

She was the happiest person
they knew.

Loved life.

A bubbly personality.

Did much charity
work.

They found her dead
last week
with slashed wrists
in her bathtub.

Apparently
there was a note.

Much
bad reading.

Sunset Red

::: AGONY :: DEATH CLUTCH :
CONFUSION SCOUNDRELS IN MANILLA WHEELBARROWS
THINKING OF COUGH SYRUP AND FLORIDA GRUPER ON
THE GRILL,
OF FACSIMILES AND SIMILES BY THEMSELVES AND ADOLPH
EICHMANN;
THE HAIRLESS NECK BRAINS OF MOJAVE
VULTURES -

and RODIN (pronounced "rodent" by my former child self)
sculpted the COCKpit in spiralling antecedent nosedive;
then he sculpted a pilot and co-pilot and stuffed them inside
like intestines,
even adding a sandwich compartment
by the fire extinguisher
(so sure his little biddies would want to eat sandwiches,
spreading orange marmalade crust to crust;
lines of longitude and butter knife preservation),
many stewardesses in blue getups
pointing to exits with helpful painted fingers,
and there's a movie playing A MOVIE PLAYING
look there: it's just like a movie playing,
except all the actors are thoughtless celery stocks
and the leading lady is a rounded candle holder
and there are tea lights for eyes
and no one has any noses
and a tiny rat of a dog in a field digs up old city by-laws
where there should be bodies
where there should be Hoffa
where there should be spit pimps with sequined switch-
blades

twisted deep in gut
where there could be the QUEEN of Spain...
Isabella or Esmeralda or Franco after gender reassignment
(that's what they call it nowadays, right? Reassignment?...
like you started in one place, then were told to be
someplace else, I like it   I like it   I like it:
there should be more gender reassignment
and less Napalm,
medium rare steaks where there used to be finish everything
on your plate earwax turnip,
more worms for the birds and birds for the cats and cats
for the couch where so-called lives go to sit
before dying).

::: CONFUSION :: AGONY CLUTCH :
DEATH SCOUNDRELS ON MERRY-GO-ROUND MARKSMEN
HOPING FOR REVERSE COWGIRL NIGHTS OF SHADOW PUP-
PET AMNESIA,
FOR COLD BEER AND WARM WOMEN DRESSED LIKE
ADOLPH EICHMANN;
THE HAIRLESS BALL SACK OF ANTARCTICA -

and my car wouldn't start and my heart threatened to stop
(all hearts do)
so I took my tire iron in hand and beat LOVE
into the pavement,
LOVE to a pulp like oranges off the truck,
and then I beat the pavement with my fists
until the pavement became all sunset red
and I sat and admired it along the dusty shoulder
as the bullfrogs all sang me Tuscan
arias
and the passing car horn erections honked their LOVE juice
all over the land,

this land
where they give their streets names
just as they do
their
children.

Endgame

There is a definite art
to playing things out,
sure you don't want to carry on
too long
like a spoiled child,
but you don't want to miss anything
either.
The devil is in the details,
they say,
it's all about the minutia.
The way long wisps
of eyebrow hair
pay bills
on silly meat grinder
heads,
the dripping vibration of running
exhaust pipes
in lonely car parks
while others run
for re-election.

I AM still
learning...
forever learning.

I AM small
and localised
and periodic table
exact.

It is Easy

to be sparse
in verse
if you are sparse
in life:

eat
sleep
drink
write
fuck.

The life
of the Spartan
3000 years
after the practice
of exposure
became frowned
upon.

Lennon Was Kinda Right

Imagine Faulkner
each night
awake in his underwear
writing poems
of Northern Aggression.

Imagine Keats
before urns,
Shelley
before the boat.

Herman Melville
with a name
that won't get you
trounced

in the
schoolyard.

I'm Just Saying

Some guy is going
around Toronto
of late
scraping out the right eyes
of cats,
always the
right.

And then there were
the beheaded birds
perched on the chain link fence
down by the old memorial centre
in Kingston
a few years back.
I used to pass them each day
as I walked home
from the Laundromat
bag slung over shoulder
and there would be more
than the day before.
All sitting beheaded
without comment.

And then there's
Michael Owen Perry
killing his whole family,
then renting five televisions
so he can watch the static,
believing Olivia Newton John
is communicating with him secretly
by changing the colour

of her eyeshade.

Or Joseph Kallinger –
the mad cobbler –
ordering his young son to rob
the women he rapes
and murders,
eventually becoming the prison cobbler
and repairing the shoes
of fellow inmates
with great proficiency.

And of course
there is you.
All of you.
And then there is me
and then some more
of you.

People are really
messed up.

Especially
all of
you.

Drawn and Quartered

It's tough slogging
like anything
else.

A real bloodbath.

Bottle into word
word in bottle.

There are many worse things
I could be doing.

Many worse things
I have done.

I won't bore you
with the
details.

Just a few more words
until I finish off
this bottle.

No Fortune Teller

The billowing smoke never stopped.

The plant ran three eight hour shifts
'round the clock.
I worked the first in the rotation
until the foreman approached me
one day soon after lunch
and informed me
that they were cutting back
and since I had the least seniority
I had to go.
I was made to hand in my laminated
timecard and uniform.
I grabbed the lock off my locker
and then I was escorted off
the premises by security.

There was a very fearful air
to the whole thing.

I had no intention of firebombing
or maiming or killing,
but they did not know
that.

They were also not aware
that my woman had cheated on me
three days earlier
and moved out
or that I was being evicted
at the end of the week

for reasons beyond
my control.

I walked some distance
down the street
from the plant
that led to the main road
with the Dae Woo dealership
on the corner.

Then I stopped
turned around
and looked
back.

The smoke was still billowing out
up into the stratosphere
with a think pulpy
wet fart
kind of stench.

Then I turned away
and walked a few blocks
east.

I didn't have to answer
to anyone or anything anywhere
anymore
and it felt great
despite the rest
of it.

This was an untruth, of course,
but it was a convenient

and necessary
one.

A small smirk stretched across my face
as I walked along
in the early afternoon
sun.

There was a bare chested middle-aged man
in bikini bottoms
with one pink heel on
coming the other
way.

The future is high
and so hard
to see,
I thought.

Reaching deep into my pocket
for my blade,
I moved
forward.

Another 3:30 in the Morning Poem

I am drunk
and in my underwear.
There is thunder now
and some lightning
a distance away.
The lights flicker
and the music slows.
I think of whip dancers in the village,
of powdered milk
and the Colossus
at Rhodes.

I wonder when the power
will go out,
how much longer
all of this
can go
on.

I Much Preferred the German Philosophers

The public library saved me.

Up Mulcaster Street
tucked away
behind city hall
across the street
from some red brick law offices
and the city jail
with its green lattice
opening.

I had to take two buses
to get there.

Pimply faced
and barely fourteen
I found the philosophers:
Heidegger, Kant, Nietzsche, Schopenhauer,
the Germans so sure of chance and will
and the irrational,
the French
every bit as sure of knowledge
and Enlightenment-era rationality,
it was fun to watch them duke it out
on the page,
no one winning
like scratch ticket hands around the gambling kiosk
in the mall,
but I much preferred the German philosophers
because they seemed so strangely demented,
old bearded ravenous minds

long dead
but blazing alive
within mine.

I could feel it.
A deep fire that no one else
seemed to have.
It was directionless,
of course,
just as liable to burn me
as anyone else,
but it saved me
from the horror of watching
my father brown bag it
with the other fathers
while their many sons
prepared for their
turn.
Just knowing there was
an alternative to the banality
of Being
meant everything.

And I voraciously thanked the philosophers
for this gift
with my
time.

And then there was space:
Copernicus, Galileo, Asimov;
theories stacked upon theories
like building blocks
to some greater realization...
and Columbus and da Gama

and Henry the Navigator
and Einstein and Tesla
and Nabokov.
Things began to get a little confused:
Joyce, Marlowe, Aquinas, Thoreau,
Hemingway, Malraux, Darwin, Jung, Huxley, Lawrence,
Milton, McLuhan, de Sade...
who said what to whom
became a blur.
I was dizzy with ideas
which seemed better
than the other.
That un-bothered unquestioning
confidence
in breakfast lunch dinner
live for work, die for country,
marry once, vote often,
do well in school because God
and/or Santa Claus
are watching
depending on the
season.
Anyways,
the librarian did not like me
at first,
but after awhile
she would smile as
she walked by the table
where I sat.

That same cream tinted table
for four years.

The good thing about

the public library –
unlike a casino
or dime slot peep
show
or something –
is that you will almost
always have your choice
of any seat
in the
house.

The restaurant goers
will go to restaurants
and the movie goers
will go to movies.

No one goes to a library
unless they absolutely
have to.

It is all very predictable
(daily life,
that is),

I learned that at a
young age.

But I still adored those grey old
German philosophers of
dried spittle
and scraggly beards.
For championing chance
and the will
so fiercely,

even though the library
closed each night
at nine,
five on Sundays,

no
exceptions.

The Only Gamble
Worth Winning
is Life

Captain Cook
never came back
from Polynesia
while I just came back
from the grocery store
with canned soup
canned peas
and fresh shallots
just put out,
but I guess
that's
luck.

No use dwelling
on who made it
and who did
not.

Tonight
I will run a bath
throw on
some Nine Inch
Nails
get drunk
below sea level

and think
nothing
of it.

As the Crickets Sing
in Tongues

He sat on the blanket
topless
struggling with
his shoes.

She was already
in the water,
splashing naked
in the moonlight.

Soon
he would know
what it felt like
to be inside
her.

Then
he would drive
her home
after curfew
make a few cursory promises
drive off
and never see
her
again.

And I Thought of French Toast

The roof and ceiling
were making out
and I thought of French toast
with syrup
of dry humps in dog parks
of fleet-footed satyrs
through clear-cut forests
of nowhere.

Someone
threw Hope in a blender
and I sat
and watched it
become carrot juice.

Humanity does all the leg work.

I just note its
idiocy.

I Still Write

I published my first poem
when I was ten years old.
In the local paper
and school
library
(awful reading)
and they made me go from classroom
to classroom
grades 1 through 8
reciting it again and again.
They even made me recite it
to the special needs kids
out in a red portable
under the rain
and tape recorded
the whole
thing.

Somewhere
there is a tape
of my ten year old self
yammering on about
nothing.

By the time
I was ushered in front
of the Kiwanis Club,
I had long forgotten
the words
and failed miserably.

My parents
made excuses.

Everyone
was disappointed.

Then
I was allowed
to be a kid
again.

No more circus tricks
for applause.

The dancing bear
into early
retirement.

There is an inherent danger
in publishing too early
or at all.

Young minds
are impressionable,
you could begin to believe
the applause.

Luckily
I've been a complete failure
each day since,
wasted talent
in the eyes of those
concerned.

I still write, of course,
usually late in the
evenings.

More for me
than them,
which is the way
it should
be.

My Friend Ian

has skin
tough as a $2 steak,
sun-cracked,
one too many Caribbean vacations,
his mother is a travel agent
and he gets discounts:
St. Thomas, Antigua, Barbados, Martinique...
he comes back with many exotic tales
or what he imagines
are exotic tales:

I saw a monkey crossing the road
with a pineapple
in its mouth

or

two men climbed a 40 ft. palm tree
with bare feet and hands
with a machete between
their teeth
and chopped me down
a fresh coconut
for the equivalent
of $1.50

or

the women, you wouldn't believe
the women...

My friend Ian is a flamer,
but he doesn't want anyone
to know it.
Perhaps he doesn't even know it.
Sometimes I think this to be
the case.

42 years old
still living with his mother,
never dated...

I guess the women
both here and in the Caribbean
are just playing really hard
to get.

Preaching to the Converted

Lorca
spoke of the *agony,*
always agony
and who am I
to argue?

oh what I have seen
what I have seen
what I have
seen!

Detente

There were four of us
around the table.

It had been a long night.

We were all drunk
and irritable
and perhaps
a little
silly.

The woman
with the unusually slight wrists
(our host)
got up
and started boiling pots of water
with nothing
in them.

Then her new man
(all barrel chest
and inked biceps)
went out to the garage
brought in a greasy wrench
wrapped in a green hand towel
and set it on the table
without comment.

There were more drinks
all 'round.

Much shared joviality
and some stories
from the past.

The other woman
(blond, full build,
in faded jeans
and purple polka dot
blouse)
reached into her purse
and produced
a can of mace.

She set it on the window sill
beside a large cream coloured moth
on the outside of the screen
that beat it wings
and seemed to want
in.

I smiled.

Then I excused myself
to the bathroom
and returned
moments later
with one bare foot
and a sock
full of pennies.

For the next few hours
we drank and toasted
and laughed at each
other's jokes,

but not too hard
because we were all
armed:

jailhouse hammer
mace
greasy wrench
boiling water.

Sitting around a table
in Northern Ontario,
drunk and tired
and hungry
at 6:23
in the morning.

Like good old friends
ready to become enemies
at a moment's
notice.

Statements

I prefer no statements
at all,
but if there must be statements,
make them grandiose
and fleeting:

the gold teeth of Atlantis
would tarnish my Acropolis mouth
full of cavities

or

slay a thousand dragons
and you may sublet
my underwear drawer
out to the emperor
of Rome

or perhaps
a real doozey
such as

car parks
are just armies
of Japanese metal
awaiting my further
instructions.

Say something,
the last one chided,
why don't you ever say

anything?...

I taught the tree squirrel
how to jump
and the polygamist
how to fuck
and there are acorns
in the grass seed ground
because I damn well
put them
there.

Gentleman's Agreement

$$$BELLHOP!,
bring me a giant gold wind tunnel
            with cavities before the filling;
fasten pipe cleaners to my wrists,
                        yellow pipe cleaners
            in the shape of
      genocide;
boil venison bones
            under the table,
      boil them down
                  to the marrow
and $$$BELLHOP!, remember this,
it is very important:
                  there is
            a good tip
                  in it
            for you

      if you use
discretion

and nurse-suckle
            the secret
      between
      us.

I Have Had Enough

I have had enough.
I turn off the television
and drop the remote
to the floor.

Hey, I was watching that!
she says from the other couch.
Turn that back
on.

I CAN'T...I REFUSE,
I say.
Everything they say
is a lie.
Every channel is a tv head
lying to me
with every breath,
I've had enough.

Of course they're lying silly,
everyone does...
now turn that back on,
I want to see what happens
next.

The tv head tells its lies
to the news people
who then look to put their own spin
on what was said
and then it is filtered through
the lie of the medium itself
so we can lie about it

when we talk to each other.
I CAN'T DO IT,
I say,
by the time it gets to me
it's already a third or forth generation
lie.

Well you can't expect everyone to just tell the truth, silly,
that would hurt our feelings
and then we'd all be sad.
Isn't it better to be happy?,
she asks.
Isn't it better to feel good
instead of knowing?

I don't need absolute truth,
I answer,
or damn near any truth at all,
I just can't take the distance involved
in generational lying.
I like my lies to be
more intimate,
surely you can understand
that.
I like when you fake orgasms
in bed
and tell me I'm the best
you've ever had
or I tell you
you don't look fat in that dress
and are a good
cook.
We don't need them, baby,
let's just lie to each other

from now
on.

She looks at me, smiles,
then grabs the remote
off the floor.

The tv heads began lying at me
again.

I get up
walk upstairs
and go to bed
without dinner.

Like a naughty child
punishing himself
and no one else.

The Real Basho

is about
a foot in length
with four paws
and a tail.

He uses a litter box
in the basement
and sleeps
nearly sixteen hours
a day.

The real Basho
is neither Japanese
nor into
renga.

He was never robbed
by bandits
on two separate
occasions
while travelling the
countryside.

The real Basho
bumps his head
up against everything
in the house.

Then he stops
and meows at me
because he is hungry

or wants attention

or
both.

She Had Accordion Doors

and stubby toes
like the rusted out spigot
of a water
tap

and window planters
on all the sills
with green shoots
sprouting out of
them

and two dogs that barked
and a yellow crock-pot under the sink

and no idea
about my lack of utility
because we'd just started
going together.

Nice Day Poem

It is a nice day out.
There is much hand holding
and birdsong.
The sun setting a fine
evening pink
as flowers in tended gardens
rest windless
and delightful.
It is quieter here
than it has been
in decades.
Even
the doorbell
dare not
speak.

It is a nice day
a nice day
a nice day...
so nice
you are left wondering
why this noose
sits around your
neck
as the chair
below your feet
wonders on four
legs

why you must always
stand so close
to the
ceiling?

As the Green Headed Mallard Wades By

There is so much posturing
and placation
out there.

So many urinals
driven to
piss.

I sit drunk
down by the water
on a park bench
this evening,
weeping.

I want to mean MY words.
I want MY words
to matter.

Grateful acknowledgement is made to the following publications where some of these poems may have appeared: *CV2, GloMag, In Between Hangovers, Outlaw Poetry Network, Punk Noir Magazine, Stanzaic Stylings, The Conclusion Magazine*

Ryan Quinn Flanagan is a Canadian-born author residing in Elliot Lake, Ontario, Canada with his wife and many bears that rifle through his garbage. His work can be found both in print and on-line in such places as: *The New York Quarterly, Evergreen Review, Ramingo's Porch, Red Fez* and *The Oklahoma Review.* This is his third book with Pski's Porch. His personal website is: http://ryanquinnflanagan.yolasite.com.

Pski's Porch Publishing was formed July 2012, to make books for people who like people who like books. We hope we have some small successes. **www.pskisporch.com.**

Pski's Porch

323 East Avenue
Lockport, NY 14094
www.pskisporch.com

www.ingramcontent.com/pod-product-compliance
Lightning Source LLC
Chambersburg PA
CBHW071206090426
42736CB00014B/2733